billy martin

Riddim: Claves of African Origin

Printed in USA • First Printing
ISBN: 978-0-9673098-4-2

Published by
Music in Motion Films Ltd
42 East Dunedin Road
Columbus, Ohio 43214 USA
web: www.musicinmotionfilms.com
email: mail@musicinmotionfilms.com

credits

This book is dedicated to percussionist, teacher, mentor, and friend, Frank Malabé. Thank you Frankie for opening doors for so many of us.

Thanks to Dan Thress, for believing in this project and having the courage to release it; John Medeski and Chris Wood who were there at the inception of the idea; all of my students; my beautiful wife Phaedra; African historical scholar John Cody Carvel; Riddim-book website designer-extraordinaire Bambang Witoradyo; my faithful-true-blue manager Liz Penta; my parents Jean and Alan for constant love and support in all my drumming endeavors, and especially, my teachers past-present and future!

Life is one big learning experience! Keep Growing!

—Billy Martin aka illy B (Oct 24, 2006)

Text, music, and music illustrations by Billy Martin. Photography and design by Dan Thress. Introduction by Billy Martin and Cody Carvel. Produced and edited by Dan Thress. Additional support provided by Roberto Barahona.

Billy Martin uses Zildjian Cymbals, Regal Tip sticks, and Attack Drum Heads.

For masterclasses, clinics, lessons, and performances visit www.billymartin.net or write to Billy Martin at P.O. Box 311 Closter, NJ 07624-0311

contents

cd tracking

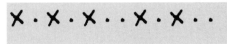

track
01

See numbers next to the examples in the book.

Track numbers correspond to music examples shaded in gray.

introduction

purpose

The purpose of this book is to bring about a deeper understanding of rhythm by studying traditional African-influenced rhythmic patterns. The language of African rhythms is a crucial step in building a vast rhythmic-vocabulary. By absorbing and mastering these African derived rhythms, you will not only enhance your musical and cultural awareness, but greatly increase your physical abilities on your instrument.

rhythmic diaspora

By studying drumming styles of West and Central Africa, it becomes clear that similarities in rhythmic expression in the Americas are a result of the Trans-Atlantic Slave Trade (see: *History of Slavery* and *The Trans-Atlantic Slave Trade* by Cody Carvel). The history, migration, and blending of cultures is an important aspect of understanding the development and phenomenon of this sophisticated language. Notes and audio recording references are included at the beginning of each chapter to illustrate the rhythmic connections between Africa and the Americas.

clave is the key

Most of my early rhythmic-based experiences originated from different African-American influences including, tap dancing, ragtime, swing, jazz, rock, funk, reggae, samba, hip-hop, etc. Within these styles I have discovered some common elements. One characteristic is the stress of rhythmic patterns signifying a key phrase within a composition or performance. This pattern is most often described as a *clave* (klä-vay) which is Spanish for **key**. *We will use the word clave to define all the key rhythmic patterns throughout this book.* Acting as a framework through the music, this cycling pattern guides the musicians and dancers.

Another key element is that these claves have two parts of equal length. These two halves act together as a *call and response* phrase and create an up-and-down motion to the rhythm. If the first part is syncopated, creating an *up-beat*, then, the other part will answer with *down-beats*. This is fundamental to understanding these claves.

The starting point of the clave phrase is determined by the "3-2" and "2-3" terminology borrowed from the Afro-Cuban tradition. This concept evolved from fundamental patterns that could be separated into two halves:

3-note section x . x . x . and 2-note section . x . x . .

3-2 x·x·x· ·x·x··   2-3 ·x·x··   x·x·x·

Throughout this book, the reader will read each clave pattern within the context of both a 3-2 and 2-3 perspective.

These claves originated from various cultures and geographical locations throughout Africa and the Americas. At the beginning of each chapter the claves are listed in *family groups* with references to its origins. Following the cultural references and list of single-line claves, each chapter concludes with a variety of polyrhythmic beats called *combinations*.

titles (disclaimer)

The names of the combinations (4 on-the-floor, jump rope, etc.) do not always correspond to one specific culture. These titles were created only to define the relationship between the clave and leading foot, for reference purposes in this book.

playing the riddims

When learning a single-line clave, use a pair of claves (two wood sticks struck together), or clapping your hands. When playing a drumset you can apply the clave pattern to a cowbell, ride cymbal or side of floor tom, and use your other hand to play the accompanying patterns.

When playing the different combinations, choose your own sounds; for example, play the accompanying hand patterns on the snare drum or toms. The accompanying foot rhythms on the hi-hat. The main thing is to be musical with your choice of sounds, tempos, dynamics and feel for each combination. If it sounds good, and feels good, you are on the right path.

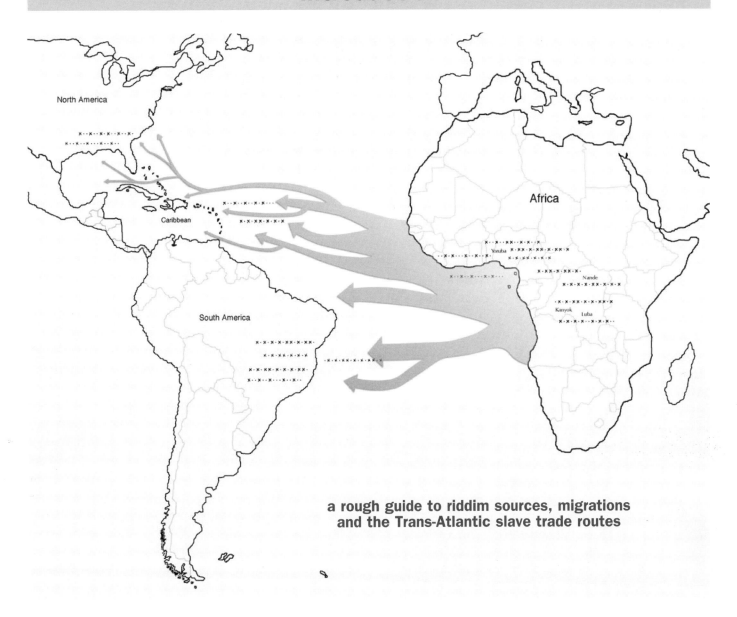

a rough guide to riddim sources, migrations and the Trans-Atlantic slave trade routes

history of slavery

There is substantial documentation of slavery throughout recorded history. The 'great' civilizations—from ancient Mesopotamia, India, China, Egypt, Greece, and Rome to the more recent empires of Western Europe—subjugated men, women, and children for use in the home, fields, market, and in battle. Ancient justifications for such enslavement varied little. The reigning gods of Mesopotamia had conquered lesser gods and created humans as a race of devoted, worshipping slaves. These humans in turn used the story of their creation to justify the enslavement of 'lesser' men: those conquered in war or who had transgressed the law. Much of the ancient world subscribed to a variation of this punitive slavery.

Though certainly not the first thinker to advocate servitude, Aristotle's justifications would be the basis for much of the western world's argument for slavery. In his Nicomachean Ethics, Aristotle defines the slave as a "living tool;" he concludes early in his Politics that slavery is "advantageous and just" for both the slave and society. Aristotle does not detail the qualifications necessary to be considered a slave, and admits that the establishment of such criteria is difficult. As the trade routes between Europe and the rest of the world expanded, so did the scientific, political, and economic justifications for free human labor. The libraries of the Enlightenment no doubt held the writings of Aristotle; and the New World, founded on the ideas of the Enlightenment would need many living tools to secure its success.

trans-atlantic slave trade

Slavery existed in Africa before European colonization of the continent and shared many of the foundations of slavery systems found elsewhere geographically and throughout history. In Africa one could be enslaved as a by product of intertribal warfare or by violating religious or tribal law. Tribes victorious in war would often enslave the defeated, adding them to the labor force of the tribe. Because many societies in Africa did not require household slaves, slavery was used to work the vast landscape for food and commodities to trade. Slaves became a part of this tradable landscape within Africa, and with the advent of European contact with the continent, these Africans would become exported commodities.

Beginning in the mid-15th Century Portugal began acquiring slaves from the western coasts of Africa to work on Portuguese sugar plantations. Portugal's control of Brazil would result in the movement of roughly five million people to the colony. Portugal would dominate the slave trade until the 17th Century when Holland would overtake both Portugal's trading posts and its domination of the slave trade. Holland would be the first colonial power to bring African slaves to what is now the United States. In the 18th Century, the English began to monopolize the slave trade. Nearly every power in Western Europe participated in the trade of Africans. The "triangular" exchange began with the trading of goods produced in Europe to Africans for African slaves. The slaves were then traded in the western colonies for goods such as cotton, sugar, and tobacco. These crops were taken back to Europe where the cycle would begin again.

It is estimated that upward of fifteen million Africans, from the present-day coasts of Senegal down to Angola, were enslaved and traded by Europeans. 80 percent of African slaves were destined for either the Caribbean islands or Brazil. Spain was responsible for sending about 15 percent of this fifteen million to its colonies in Central and South America.

Only about five percent of slaves from Africa were sent to the present-day United States. Olaudah Equiano, enslaved in the 17th Century in what is now Nigeria describes the slave ship as "filled with horrors of every kind." Death rates were high and suicides were common on the ships headed to the Americas; these rates did not drop dramatically upon arrival at the plantations. Any attempt to improve upon the aggregate numbers concerning slavery in the Americas is a statistical formality. There will never be an accurate tally of the lives affected by the Trans-Atlantic slave trade. Countless families were ravaged in the name of profit and countless lives lost in the name of material production. Guilt and fear have survived the diaspora; we are thankful that the art, literature, religion, and music of the African cultures have proved impossible to enslave and live on.

riddim notation

interpreting the notation

The following page contains the key for understanding the symbols used to notate the rhythms in this book. It is important to remember that this system is open to interpretations in sound choices, tempos, phrasing and dynamics.

single-line clave

Simply tap out the rhythm and remember that the sound (x) and space (.) are of equal time value. Repeat the line without pausing.

✗ = sound   • = space

✗ · ✗ · ✗ · · ✗ · ✗ · ·

---

clave and foot combination

If you are right-handed, generally speaking, your right hand will be your lead-hand. In this case the lead-hand is playing the clave (on cowbell, ride cymbal bell, side of the floor tom, etc.). The lead foot signifies the bass drum. Each rhythm can be orchestrated to fit the player's style. I use the term *voicings* when selecting my own sounds for each rhythm.

lead hand

lead foot

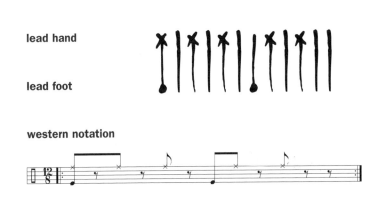

western notation

---

adding the accompanying hand

In this example, we add a counter-rhythm with our other hand. The upper notes indicate the high drum and the lower notes indicate the low drum. Drumset players can use high and low toms. Variations include substituting a cross-stick on the snare or muting tones on the drums. The notation remains the same. Listen for variations on the CD.

Percussionists can use congas, timbales or other high and low sounds.

accompanying hand

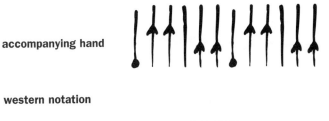

western notation

---

adding the accompanying foot

In this example we add a counter-rhythm (accompanying pattern) with our other foot. Drumset players can use the hi-hat. Percussionists can try tapping their foot or playing with bells attached to the ankle.

accompanying foot

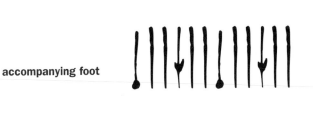

western notation

riddim references

Afro-Claves In Six are deeply rooted Yoruban rhythms from West
and Central Africa, the Caribbean, and the Americas.

𝗫 · 𝗫 · 𝗫 · · 𝗫 · 𝗫 · ·

Central African Republic / *Central African Republic: Aka Pygmies* / "Hunting Songs" / (Auvdis)
Cuba / *Orishas Across The Ocean: The Yoruba Dahomean Collection* / "Song for Nana Buruku" (Ryko)

𝗫 · 𝗫 · 𝗫 · 𝗫𝗫 · 𝗫 · 𝗫

Ghana, West Africa / *Rhythms of Life, Songs of Wisdom* / "Akan Fontom from Adzewa" (Smithsonian Folkways/eMusic.com)
Haiti, Caribbean / *Rhythms of Rapture: Sacred Musics of Haitian Voodou* / "Simbi Dio" (Smithsonian Folkways/eMusic.com)
Matanzas, Cuba / *Afro-Cuban Sacred Music from the Countryside* / "Shango Moforibale; Yele; Toque Yesa for Oshun"

𝗫 · 𝗫 · 𝗫𝗫 · 𝗫 · 𝗫 · 𝗫

Togo, West Africa / *Togo: Music From West Africa* / "Unayafame" (Rounder)
Ghana, West Africa / *Master Drummers of Dagbon, Vol.1* / "Yoruba-Waa" (Rounder)
Havana, Cuba / *Orishas Across The Ocean: The Yoruba Dahomean Collection* / "Song for Yemaya" (Ryko)
Matanzas, Cuba / *Los Muñequitos De Matanzas* / "Congo Yambumba" (Qbadisc)
Cuba / *Afro-Cuba: A Musical Anthology* / "Song For Ogun" (Rounder)
Cuba / *Africa in America* / "Canto a Chango" (Discos Corason)
Cuba / *Cachao y su Conjunto: Descarga* / "Criolla Carabali" (Maype)
USA / *Max Roach: Percussion Bitter Suite* / "Garvey's Ghost" (Impulse)

𝗫 · 𝗫 · 𝗫𝗫 · 𝗫 · 𝗫𝗫 ·

Ghana / *Master Drummers of Dagbon Vol.1* / "Gaabiti Zamanduniya" (Rounder)
Malawi, Southern Central Africa / *Traditional Music of Malawi* / Track 17
Salvador, Bahia, Brazil / *Orishas Across The Ocean: The Yoruba Dahomean Collection* / "Ketu: Roda de Dada" (Ryko)

𝗫 · 𝗫 · 𝗫 · 𝗫𝗫 · 𝗫𝗫 ·

Matanzas, Cuba / *Afro-Cuban Sacred Music from the Countryside* / "Ibarabo Ago Mo Juba, Song for Elegua" (Smithsonian Folkways)

𝗫 · 𝗫 · · 𝗫 · 𝗫 · 𝗫 · ·

Central African Republic / *Central African Republic: Music of the Former Banda Courts* / Track 12
Benin, West Africa / *Benin: Rythmes Et Chants Pour Les Vodun* / "Rythme Nago—Yoruba" (VDE-Gallo)
Matanzas, Cuba / *Los Munequitos De Matanzas* / "Abacua"
Cuba / *Los Munequitos De Matanzas: Guaguanco Columbia Yambu* / "Cacho" (Vitral)
Cuba / *Afro-Cuba—A Musical Anthology* / "Salida Efi" (Rounder)

𝗫 · 𝗫𝗫 · 𝗫 · 𝗫𝗫 · 𝗫 ·

Cuba / *Cuba: Bata, Bembe and Palo Songs* / "Ago ago, Songs for Eshu" (Smithsonian Folkways/eMusic.com)

afro-claves in six

track 01	**3-2 claves**	track 02	**2-3 claves**

1
3-2: X · X · X · · X · X · ·
2-3: · X · X · · X · X · X ·

2
3-2: X · X · X · · X · X · X
2-3: · X · X · X X · X · X ·

3
3-2: X · X · X · X X · X · X
2-3: X X · X · X X · X · X ·

4
3-2: X · X · X X · X · X · X
2-3: · X · X · X X · X · X X

5
3-2: X · X · X X · X · X · ·
2-3: · X · X · · X · X · X X

6
3-2: X · X · X X · X · X X ·
2-3: · X · X X · X · X · X X

7
3-2: X · X · X · X X · X X ·
2-3: X X · X X · X · X · X ·

8
3-2: X · X · · X · X · X · ·
2-3: · X · X · · X · X · · X

9
3-2: X · X X · X · X · X X ·
2-3: · X · X X · X · X X · X

10
3-2: X · X X · X · X X · X ·
2-3: · X X · X · X · X X · X

11
3-2: · · X · X · · X · X · X
2-3: · X · X · X · · · X · X

3-2 afro-claves in six

"2 on-the-floor"

tracks
03/04

1

2

7

3

8

4

9

5

10

6

11

---

accompanying foot

1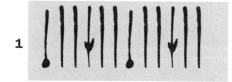

2

3

accompanying hand

1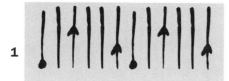

2

3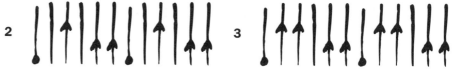

2-3 afro-claves in six

"2 on-the-floor"

tracks
05/06

1

2

7

3

8

4

9

5

10

6

11

---

accompanying foot

1

2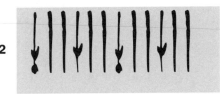

3

accompanying hand

1

2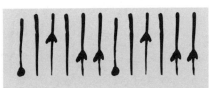

3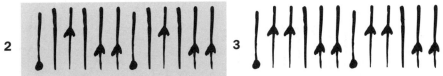

11

3-2 afro-claves in six

"4 on-the-floor"

tracks 07/08

1

2

7

3

8

4

9

5

10

6

11

accompanying foot

1

2

3

accompanying hand

1

2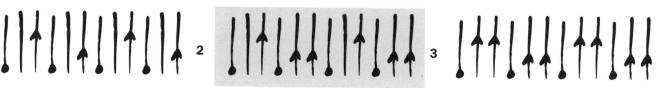

3

12

2-3 afro-claves in six

"4 on-the-floor"

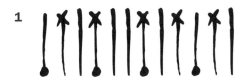

1

2

7

3

8

4

9

5

10

6

11

accompanying foot

1   2   3

accompanying hand

1   2   3

13

3-2 afro-claves in six

"skip in two"

track 09

1

2    7

3    8

4 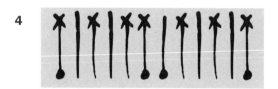   9

   10

6    11

---

accompanying foot

accompanying hand

14

2-3 afro-claves in six

"skip in two"

tracks
10/11

1

2

7

3

8

4

9

5

10

6

11

---

accompanying foot

   2    3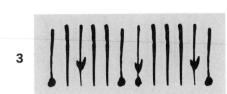

accompanying hand

1 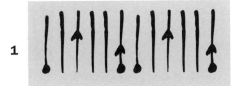   2    3

15

3-2 afro-claves in six

"3 on-the-floor"

tracks 12/13

1   

2   7   

3   8   

4   9   

5   10   

6   11   

accompanying foot

1    2    3

accompanying hand

1    2    3

16

2-3 afro-claves in six

"3 on-the-floor"

1

2

7

3

8

4

9

5

10

6

11

accompanying foot

1 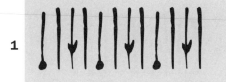   2    3

accompanying hand

1 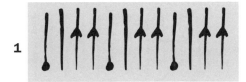   2    3

17

3-2 afro-claves in six

"samba in 3"

tracks
15/16

1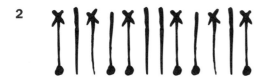

2    7

3    8

4 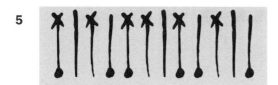   9

5    10

6 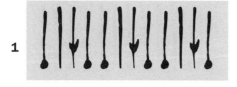   11

---

accompanying foot

1    2   3

accompanying hand

1    2    3

2-3 afro-claves in six

"samba in 3"

1

2

7

3

8

4

9

5

10

6

11

accompanying foot

accompanying hand

19

3-2 afro-claves in six

"3 off-the-floor"

1

2

3

4

5

6

7

8

9

10

11

---

accompanying foot

1 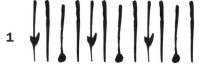   **2**    **3**

accompanying hand

1    **2** 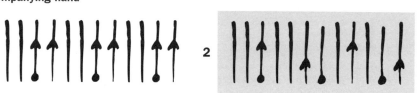   **3**

2-3 afro-claves in six

"3 off-the-floor"

1

2

7

3

8

4

9

5

10

6

11

accompanying foot

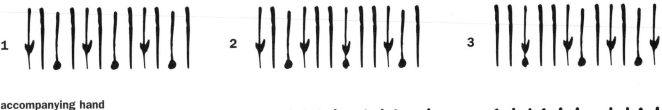
1   2   3

accompanying hand

1   2   3

"6 on-the-floor"

1

2    7

3    8

4    9

5    10

6    11

accompanying foot

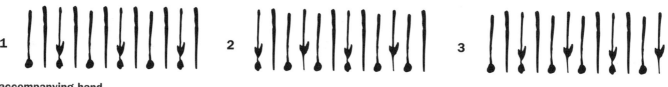

accompanying hand

2-3 afro-claves in six

"6 on-the-floor"

tracks
19/20

1

2

7

3

8

4

9

5

10

6

11

accompanying foot

1  2 3

accompanying hand

1  2 3

23

3-2 afro-claves in six

"4 doubles bd"

1

2

3

4

5

6

7

8

9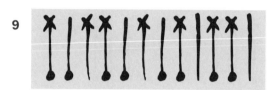

10

11

---

accompanying foot

1  2 3

accompanying hand

1 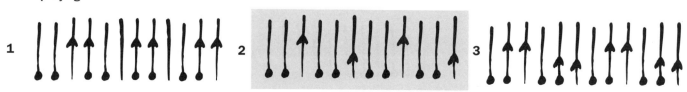 2 3

2-3 afro-claves in six

"4 doubles bd"

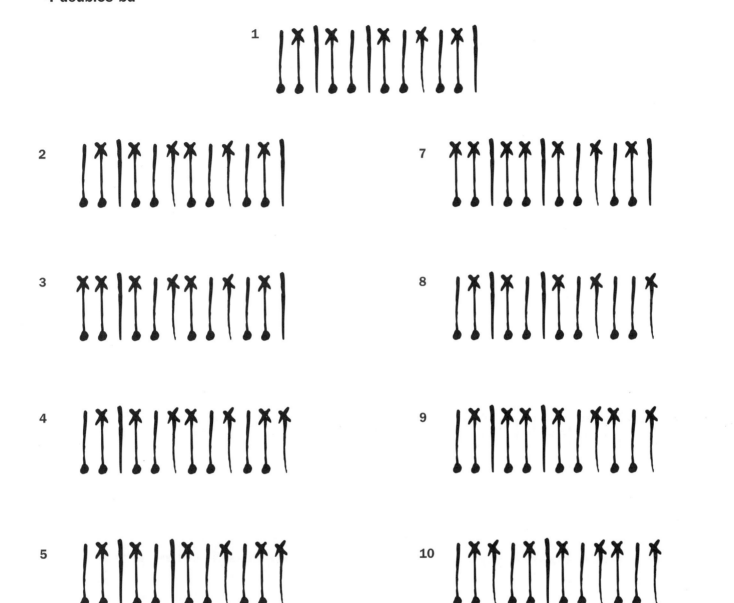

accompanying foot

accompanying hand

3-2 afro-claves in six

"3 doubles bd"

track 23

1

2

7

3

8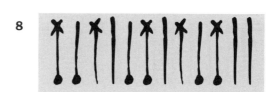

4

9

5

10

6

11

---

accompanying foot

accompanying hand

2-3 afro-claves in six

"3 doubles bd"

1

2

7

3

8

4

9

5

10

6

11

accompanying foot

accompanying hand

3-2 afro-claves in six

"2 doubles bd"

track
24

1

2    7

3    8

4    9

5    10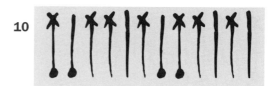

6    11

---

accompanying foot

1 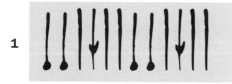   2    3

accompanying foot

1 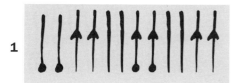   2    3

2-3 afro-claves in six

"2 doubles bd"

1

2

7

3

8

4

9

5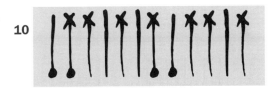

10

6

11

accompanying foot

1  2  3

accompanying hand

1 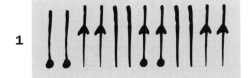 2  3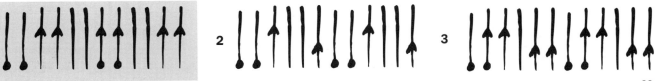

3-2 afro-claves in six [part two]
"waltz feet"

1

2

3

4

5

6

7

8

9

10

11

accompanying hand

1

2

3

2-3 afro-claves in six [part two]

"waltz feet"

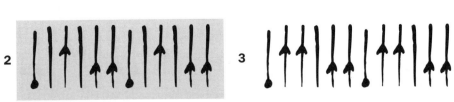

accompanying hand

3-2 afro-claves in six [part 2]

"waltz feet 2"

accompanying hand

2-3 afro-claves in six [part 2]

"waltz feet 2"

track 27

1

2

7

3

8

4

9

5

10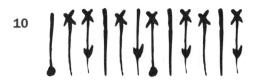

6

11

---

accompanying hand

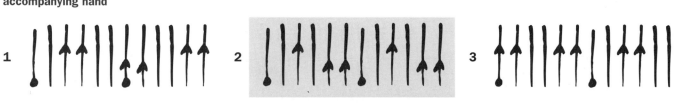

1   2   3

"4 feet"

1

2

7

3

8

4

9

5

10

6

11

accompanying hand

1

2    7

3    8

4    9

5    10

6    11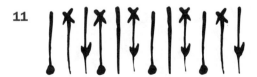

accompanying hand

"jump rope"

1

2

7

3

8

4

9

5

10

6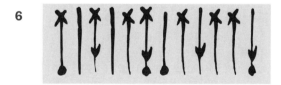

11

accompanying hand

1 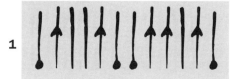 2  3

2-3 afro-claves in six [part 2]

"jump rope"

track
29

1

2    7

3    8

4    9

5    10

6 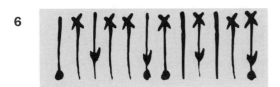   11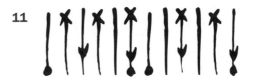

accompanying hand

3-2 afro-claves in six [part 2]

"4+3 on-the-floor"

track 30

1

2

7

3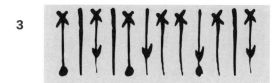

8

4

9

5

10

6

11

accompanying hand

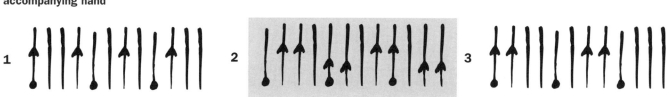

1   2   3

38

"4+3 on-the-floor"

1

2    7

3    8

4    9

5    10

6    11

---

accompanying hand

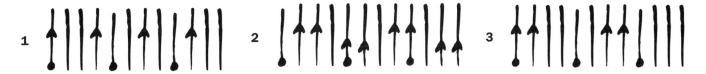

"samba in 3 against 4"

track 31

1

2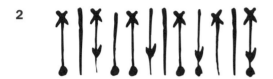

7

3

8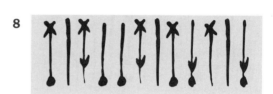

4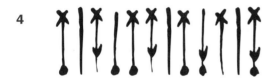

9

5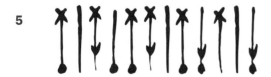

10

6

11

accompanying hand

1  2 3

"samba in 3 against 4"

track
32

1

2

7

3

8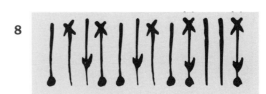

4

9

5

10

6

11

accompanying hand

1  2  3

"4+3 off-the-floor"

1

2    7

3   8

4   9

5   10

6   11

accompanying hand

1 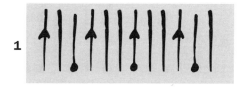   2    3

"4+3 off-the-floor"

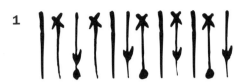

1

2  7

3  8

4  9

5 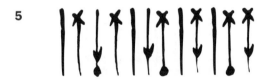 10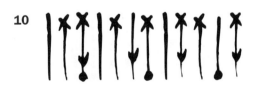

6 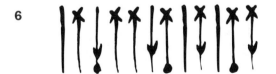 11

accompanying hand

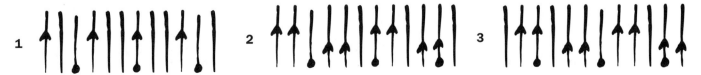

"4+6 on-the-floor"

track
34

1

2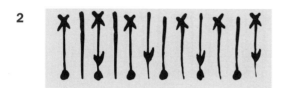

7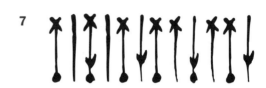

3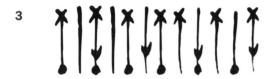

8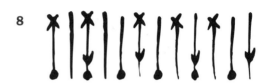

4

9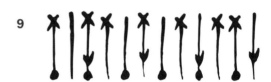

5

10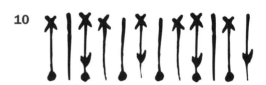

6

11

accompanying hand

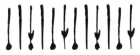

2-3 afro-claves in six [part 2]

"4+6 on-the-floor"

track
35

1

2
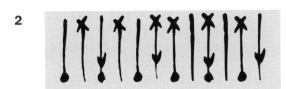

7

3

8

4

9
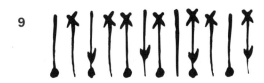

5

10
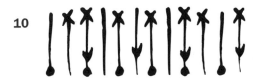

6

11

accompanying hand

1   2   3

riddim references

Afro-Claves in Four closely resemble the Afro-Claves in Six and have strong Yoruban connections from West and Central Africa into the Caribbean, and the Americas. Switching phrasing from a "six" to "four," and "four" to "six" are commonplace in Yoruban music.

X · · X · · X · · · X · X · · ·

Benin, West Africa, Yoruban / *Benin: Rythmes et chants pour les vodun* / "Nago" (VDE)
Ghana, West Africa / *Drums of Death* / "Parago" (Avant)
Salvador, Bahia, Brazil / *Orishas Across The Ocean: The Yoruba Dahomean Collection* / "Opanije—Rhythms for Omolu" (Ryko)
Brazil / *Olodum* / Track 3 (Soundware)
New York City, USA / *A Tribe Called Quest: The Low End Theory* / Check The Rhime (Jive)

X · · X · · X · · · X · · X · ·

Brazil / *Luiz Bonfa: Le Roi de la Bossa Nova* / "Cantiga Da Vida; Amor Por Amor" (emusic.com)
Brazil / *Antonio Carlos Jobim: The Man from Ipanema* / "O Morro Nao Tem Vez; Meditacao" (Verve)
Brazil / *Luciano Perrone: Batucada Fantastica—Os Ritmistas Brasileiros* / "Marcha de Carnaval; Reco-Reco 2"

X · · X · · X X · · X · X · · X

Nigeria / *Elewe Music and Dance* / "Elewe-Yoruba" (Smithsonian Folkways/emusic.com)

X · · X · · · X · · X · X · · ·

Cuba / *Africa in America* / "Columbia–Cuba–Recuerdo A Malanga" (Discos Corason)
Ghana / *Master Drummers of Dagbon Vol. 1* / "Amajiro" (Rounder)
Togo / *Togo: Music From West Africa* / "Ki Man Wo–Ali Bawa" (Rounder)

X · · X · · · X · · X · X · · ·　　　　　**· · X · X · · · X · · X · · · X**

Cuba / *Los Munequitos De Matanzas: Guaguanco Columbia Yambu* / "Congo Yambumba" (Vitral 277)

X · X X · X · X X · X · X X · X

Nigeria / *King Sunny Ade and His African Beats: The Rough Guide to the Music of Nigeria and Ghana* / "Maa Jo" (World Music Network)

3-2 claves   **2-3 claves**

#	3-2 claves	2-3 claves
1	X · · X · · X · · · X · X · · ·	· · X · X · · · X · · X · · X ·
2	X · · X · · X · · · X · · X · ·	· · X · · X · · X · · X · · X ·
3	X · · X · · · X · · X · X · · ·	· · X · X · · · X · · X · · · X
4	X · · X · · X X · · X · X · · X	· · X · X · · X X · · X · · X X
5	X · X X · X X · X · X · X X · X	X · X · X X · X X · X X · X X ·
6	X X · X X X · X X · X · X X · X	X · X · X X · X X X · X X X · X
7	X · X X · X · X X · X · afro · X	X · X · X X · X X · X X · X · X
8	· X X X · X · X X · X · X X X X	X · X · X X X X · X X X · X · X
9	X · · X · X · · X · X · · X · ·	X · X · · X · · X · · X · X · ·

"2 on-the-floor"

1

2

6

3

7

4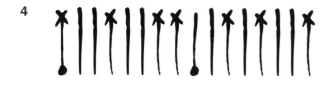

8

5

9

accompanying foot

1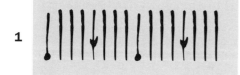

2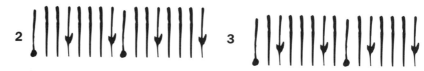

3

accompanying hand

1

2

3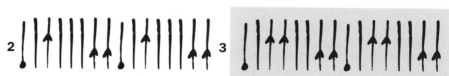

3-2 afro-claves in four

"2 on-the-floor"

1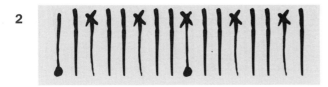

2

6

3

7

4

8

5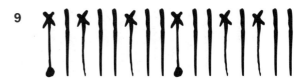

9

---

accompanying foot

1    2    3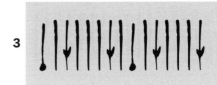

accompanying hand

1    2 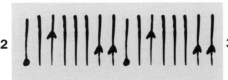   3

3-2 afro-claves in four

"4 on-the-floor"

**tracks
40/41**

1   *(rhythm notation)*

2

6

3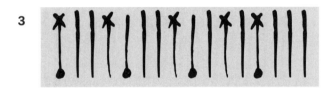

7

4 *(rhythm notation)*

8

5 *(rhythm notation)*

9

---

accompanying foot

1    2 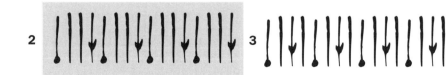   3

accompanying hand

1    2   3

50

2-3 afro-claves in four

"4 on-the-floor"

1   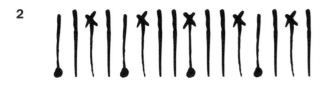

2      6   

3   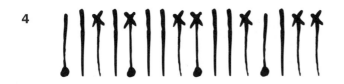   7   

4      8   

5   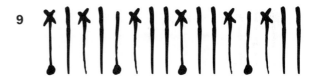   9

---

accompanying foot

1   2   3 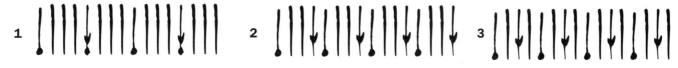

accompanying hand

1   2   3 

3-2 afro-claves in four

"2 off-the-floor"

track 42

1

2

6

3

7

4

8

5

9

---

accompanying foot

1

2

3

accompanying hand

1

2

3

2-3 afro-claves in four

"2 off-the-floor"

3-2 afro-claves in four

"skip in two"

tracks 44/45

1

2
6

3
7

4
8

5
9

accompanying foot

1
2
3

accompanying hand

1
2
3

54

2-3 afro-claves in four

"skip in two"

1   

2

3

4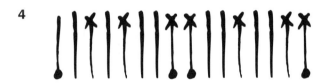

5

6

7

8

9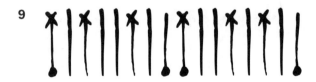

---

accompanying foot

accompanying hand

3-2 afro-claves in four

"samba nova"

1

2

3

4

5

6

7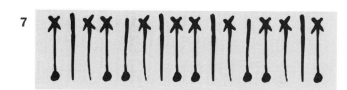

8

9

---

accompanying foot

1  2 3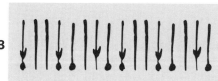

accompanying hand

1  2 3

2-3 afro-claves in four

"samba nova"

1

2

6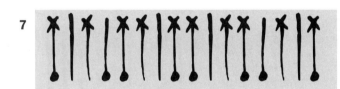

3

7

4

8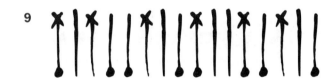

5

9

---

accompanying foot

1  2 3

accompanying hand

1 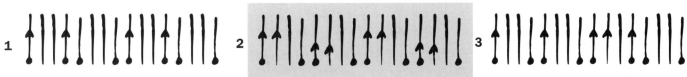 2 3

3-2 afro-claves in four

"tumbao"

1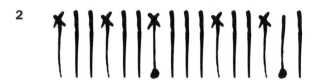

2

6

3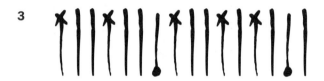

7

4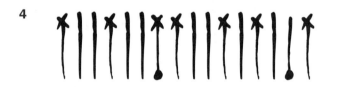

8

5

9

---

accompanying foot

1   2   3
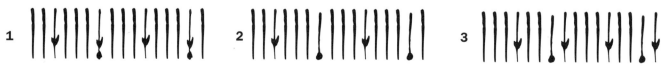

accompanying hand

1   2   3
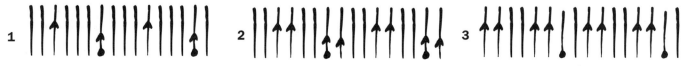

58

2-3 afro-claves in four

"tumbao"

1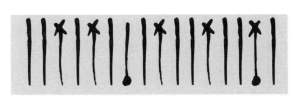

2

6

3

7

4

8

5

9

---

accompanying foot

1 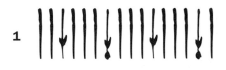   2   3

accompanying hand

1    2 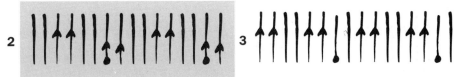   3

59

"guaguanson"

track
50

1

2   6

3   7

4   8

5   9

accompanying foot

accompanying hand

2-3 afro-claves in four

"guaguanson"

1

2

6

3

7

4

8

5

9

---

accompanying foot

1

2

3

accompanying hand

1

2

3

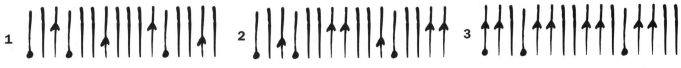

3-2 afro-claves in four

"songo bd"

tracks 52/53

1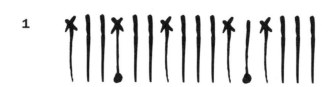

2   6

3   7

4   8

5   9

---

accompanying foot

1 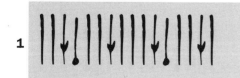   2    3

accompanying hand

1   2 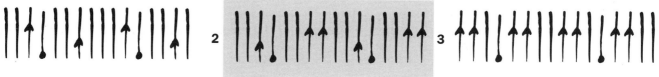   3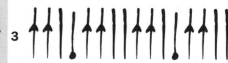

2-3 afro-claves in four

"songo bd"

tracks
54/55

1

2

6

3

7

4

8

5

9

---

accompanying foot

1

2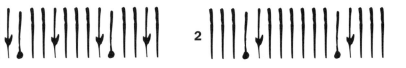

3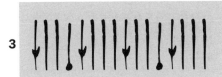

accompanying hand

1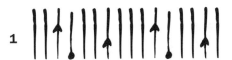

2

3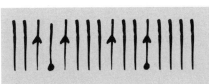

3-2 afro-claves in four

"charleston bd"

1

2

6

3

7

4

8

5

9

---

accompanying foot

1

2

3

accompanying hand

1

2

3

2-3 afro-claves in four

"charleston bd"

1

2

6

3

7

4

8

5

9

accompanying foot

1  2 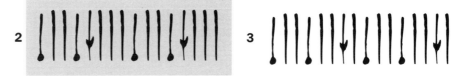 3

accompanying hand

1  2 3

65

3-2 afro-claves in four

"baiao bd"

tracks
57/58

1

2

6

3

7

4

8

5

9

---

accompanying foot

1 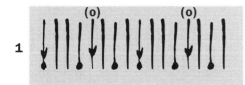   **2**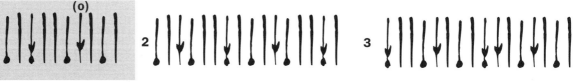

accompanying foot

1    **2**

2-3 afro-claves in four

"baiao bd"

1

2  6

3  7

4  8

5  9

---

accompanying foot

accompanying hand

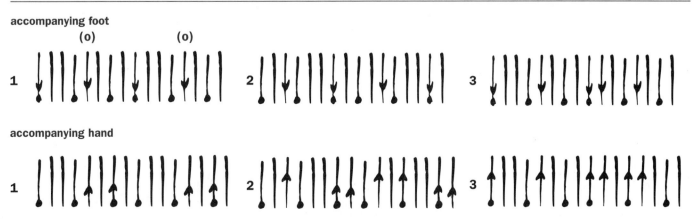

riddim references

Afro-claves in eight are commonly used in Brazilian Samba,
Batucada and Bossa Nova music, as well as throughout
Central Africa where these patterns dominate rural and urban
cultures past and present.

X · X · X · X · · X · X · X · ·

Congo / *Congo 1952 & 1957; Kanyok and Luba* / "Chindol Wa Mukaleng" and "Musambo Wa Maja"
Zaire / *Zaire-Luba-Shankadi du Shaba: Tombe Ditumba* / "Dikembe" (Fonti Musicali)

X · X · X · X · XX · X · X · X

Zaire / *Zaire: La Musique des Nande* / "Guitare" (VDE)
Zaire / *Musiques Urbaines a Kinshasa* / "Rhythm Kuatankuaka" (Ocora)

X · X · XX · X · X · X · XX ·

Brazil / *Escola de Samba da Cidade e Paulino sua Bateria* / Partido Alto
Brazil / *Luciano Perrone: Batucada Fantastica- Brazilian Rhythms* / Cuica

X · X · X · · X · X · X · XX ·

Brazil / *Luciano Perrone: Batucada Fantastica- Brazilian Rhythms* / Tamborims and Prato e Faca, etc.

· X · X · XX · X · X · XX · X

Brazil / *Teresa Christina E Grupo Semente: A Música De Paulinho da Viola 2* / Argumento

X · X · XX · XX · XX · X · X

Congo, Zaire, Central Africa / *Zaire: La Musique des Nande* / "Guitare" (VDE)
Cuba / *Cachao Y Su Orchestra: Jam Session with Feeling* / "Redencion" (Maype)

X · X · XX · X · X · XX · X ·

Zaire / *Zaire-Luba-Shankadi du Shaba: Tombe Ditumba* / "Kinkondja; Ditumba Matolo" (Fonti Musicali)
Congo / *Congo 1952 & 1957 : Kanyok & Luba* / Mal' Yoo-Yooy

XX · X · X · XX · X · X · X ·

Congo / **Congo 1952 & 1957 : Kanyok & Luba** / *Bwal Bwany*

afro-claves in two

Music and dance styles around the world with names like soca,
soukous, highlife, second line, and reggaeton are based on these
patterns. (see pages 86-87)

X · · X · · X ·

Matanzas, Cuba / *Orishas Across The Ocean: The Yoruba Dahomean Collection* / "Ochun Talade" (Ryko 10405)
Central Africa / *Afrique Central: Tambours Kongo* / Kambanu Papa; Nkuanga; Trompe an corne de bovide (Buda)
New Orleans, USA / *Baby Dodds Trio: Jazz a'la Creole* / "Tootie Ma" (GHB)

X · XX · XX ·

Central African Republic / *Nbaka Peoples* / *Central African Republic* / "Song For Ancestor's Souls" (Auvdis)

afro-claves in eight

3-2 claves

2-3 claves

#	3-2 claves	2-3 claves
1	· X · X · · X · X · X · X · · X	X · X · X · · X · X · X · · X ·
2	· X · X · X X · X · X · X · · X	X · X · X · · X · X · X · X X ·
3	· X · · X · X · X · X · · X · X	X · X · · X · X · X · · X · X ·
4	· X · X · · X · X · X · X · X ·	X · X · X · X · · X · X · · X ·
5	· X · X · X · · X · X · X · X ·	X · X · X · X · · X · X · X · ·
6	· X · X · X X · X · X · X X · X	X · X · X X · X · X · X · X X ·
7	X X · X · X · X X · X · X · X ·	X · X · X · X · X X · X · X · X
8	X · X X · X · X X · X · X X · X	X · X · X X · X X · X X · X · X
9	· X · X X · X · X · X · X X · X	X · X · X X · X · X · X X · X ·

"2 on-the-floor"

1

2

6

3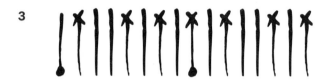

7

4

8

5

9

accompanying foot

1    2    3

accompanying hand

1    2    3

2-3 afro-claves in eight

"2 on-the-floor"

tracks
61/62

1

2

6

3

7

4

8

5

9

---

accompanying foot

1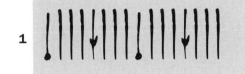

2

3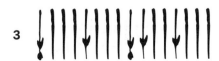

accompanying hand

1

2

3

3-2 afro-claves in eight

"4 on-the-floor"

1

2    6

3    7

4    8

5    9

---

accompanying foot

1   2   3

accompanying hand

1   2   3

2-3 afro-claves in eight

"4 on-the-floor"

tracks
63/64

1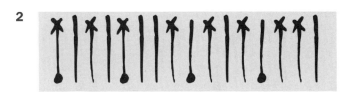

2
6

3
7

4
8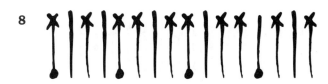

5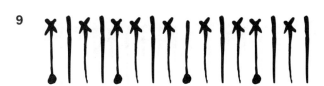
9

accompanying foot

1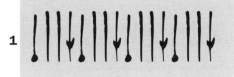
2
3

accompanying hand

1
2
3

3-2 afro-claves in eight

"2 off-the-floor"

1

2

6

3

7

4

8

5

9

---

accompanying foot

accompanying hand

2-3 afro-claves in eight

"2 off-the-floor"

tracks 65/66

1

2

6

3

7

4

8

5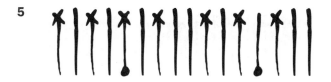

9

accompanying foot

1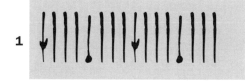

2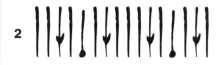

3

accompanying hand

1

2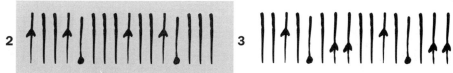

3

3-2 afro-claves in eight

"skip in 2"

1

2    6

3 ...   7 ...

4 ...   8 ...

5 ...   9 ...

accompanying foot

1 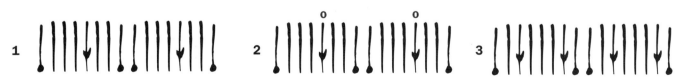   2   3

accompanying hand

1    2   3

tracks
67/68

1

2

6

3

7

4

8

5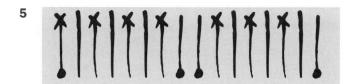

9

accompanying foot

1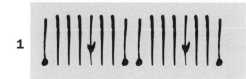

2

accompanying hand

1

2

3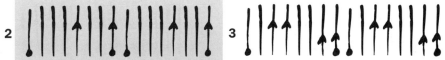

3-2 afro-claves in eight

"sambossa"

1

2

6

3

7

4

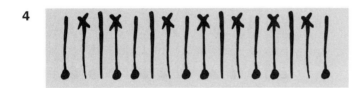

8

5

9

accompanying foot

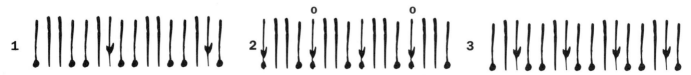

1   2   3

accompanying hand

1   2   3

2-3 afro-claves in eight

"sambossa"

1

2

6

3

7

4

8

5

9

---

accompanying foot

1 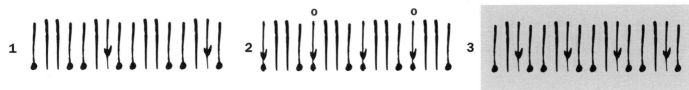 2 3

accompanying hand

1  2 3

3-2 afro-claves in eight

"charleston bd"

1

2
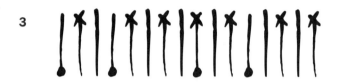

6
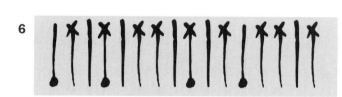

3
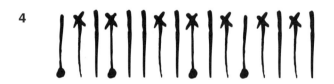

7

4

8

5

9

---

accompanying foot

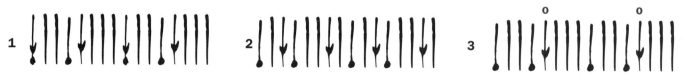

1   2   3

accompanying hand

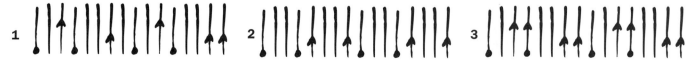

1   2   3

2-3 afro-claves in eight

"charleston bd"

1

2  6

3  7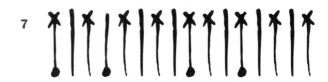

4  8

5  9

---

accompanying foot

accompanying hand

"baiao bd"

track
72

1

2

6

3

7

4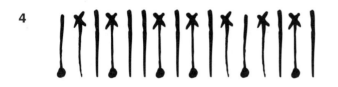

8

5

9

accompanying foot

accompanying hand

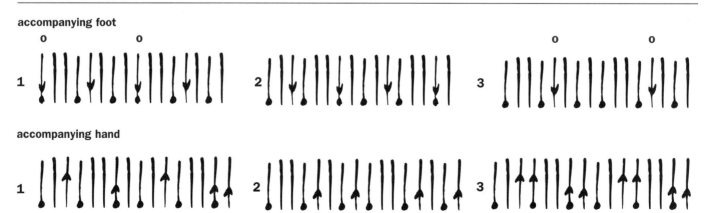

2-3 afro-claves in eight

"baiao bd"

track 73

1

2

6

3

7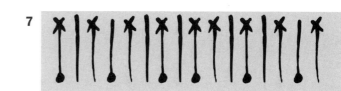

4

8

5

9

accompanying foot

accompanying hand

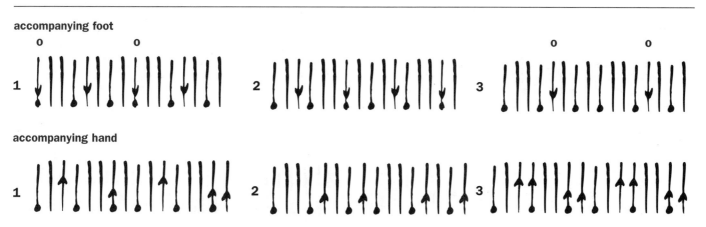

3-2 afro-claves in eight

"baiao bd variation"

1

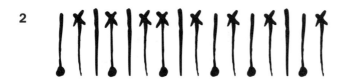

2   6

3  7

4  8

5  9

---

accompanying foot

accompanying hand

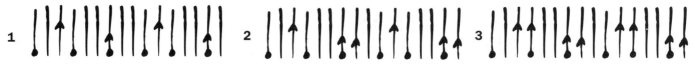

2-3 afro-claves in eight

"baiao bd variation"

1

2

6

3

7
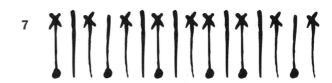

4

8
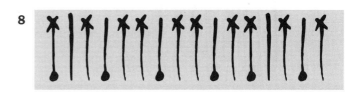

5

9

---

accompanying foot

1
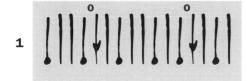

2

3

accompanying hand

1

2

3

soca

"bd variations"

track
76

1

This pattern is widespread in African cultures, especially more recent dance styles like Soca, Soukous, Highlife, New Orleans beats, Hip-Hop and Reggaeton.

2

6

3

7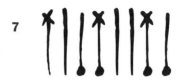

4

8

5

9

---

accompanying foot

1
2
3

accompanying hand

1
2
3

cinquillo

"bd variations"

track 77

This Caribbean rhythm used in the music of Haiti, Cuba, the Dominican Republic, and Trinidad can also be heard in the central African regions (Congo, Central African Republic, Zaire). Its five-note pattern (thus the Spanish name **cinquillo** after cinco, or five) is the characteristic rhythm of the danzón (Cuba).

1

2

3

4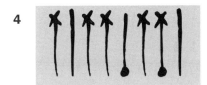

5

6

7

8

9

---

accompanying foot

1 **2** **3**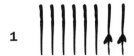

accompanying hand

1 **2** **3**

odd claves • claves in five

Common subdivisions of five are 2+3 or 3+2

1   X X · X ·

4   · X · X ·

2   X · X · X

5   X · X X ·

3   · X X · X

6   · X · X X

claves in five

1   *[claves notation]*   **tracks 78/79**

4   *[claves notation]*

2   *[claves notation]*

5   *[claves notation]*

3   *[claves notation]*

6   *[claves notation]*

hi-hat/accompanying hand

1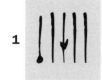

2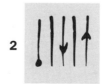

88

claves in five

1

4

2

5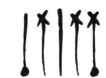

3

6

1

4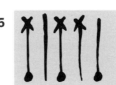

2

track 80

5

3

6

---

hi-hat/accompanying hand

1   **2**   **3**   **4**

claves in seven

Common subdivisions for seven are 2+2+3, 2+3+2 or 3+2+2

1   ✗ · ✗ · ✗ · ·

2   ✗ · · ✗ ✗ · ·

3   · ✗ · ✗ · ✗ ·

4   · ✗ · ✗ · ✗ ✗

5   ✗ · ✗ · ✗ · ✗

6   ✗ ✗ · · ✗ ✗ ·

7   ✗ ✗ · ✗ · ✗ ·

8   · ✗ · ✗ · · ✗

1

track
81

5

2

6

3

7

4

8

hi-hat

1

2

claves in seven

1

2

3 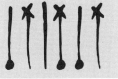   track 82

4

5

6

7

8

1

2

3

4

5

6

7

8 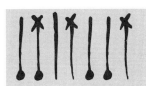   track 83

hi-hat/accompanying hand

1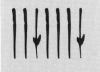

2

91

claves in ten

**tracks
84/85**

Common subdivisions for ten are
two groups of five.

1

6

2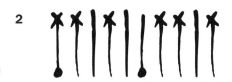

7

3

8

4

9

5

10

---

hi-hat/accompanying hand

1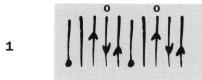

2

3

92

claves in ten

tracks
86/87

1

6

2

7

3

8

4

9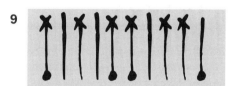

5

10

hi-hat/accompanying hand

1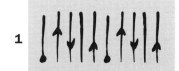

2

AFRICAN RHYTHMS AND INDEPENDENCE FOR DRUMSET
by MOKHTAR SAMBA

A revolutionary guide to applying rhythms from North Africa, Cameroon, Guinea/Mali and Senegal to the DRUMSET!

Mokhtar Samba and his explosive drumming can be heard throughout the world on tours and recordings with Salief Keita, Youssou N'Dour, Henri Dikongue, Carlinhos Brown, Richard Bona, Tama, Ultramarine, Joe Zawinul, Graham Haynes, Nguyen Le, Jean-Luc Ponty, and many others. Mokhtar's Moroccan-Senegalese heritage mixed with the jazz and Afro-fusion atmosphere of Paris has created one of the most exciting drummers of all time.

Designed for student and professional drummers interested in exploring the roots of drumming while learning new rhythms applicable to all forms of modern music, including Afro-Cuban, Brazilian, jazz, rock and funk.

CHAPTERS: Gnawa (North Africa), Maghreb (North Africa), Mangambe (Cameroon), Bikutsi (Cameroon), Doudoumba (Guinea & Mali) Sabar (Senegal).

DENNIS CHAMBERS, "This is the best explanation of African rhythms that I've heard. I really love the way Mokhtar breaks everything down and presents it to you. I like the way he plays and thinks when he's behind a drumset."

VINNIE COLAIUTA, "The grooves just LEAP off the page! Mokhtar Samba's illustrations of African Rhythm's are wonderfully insightful, enriching, and masterfully. Thank you, Mohktar for enlightening all of us!"

WILL KENNEDY, "Mokhtar has opened my mind to rhythms I have never imagined before. The more I listen, and try to incorporate them into my playing, the more I realize that I am tapping into a source of rhythmic ideas that will never run dry."

JAMEY HADDAD, "African Rhythms and Independence brings the traditional trap player into the land of the original swing —Africa—by spelling out the essentials on the set. Any broad-based analysis of a continent's worth of drumming is an ambitious work, but Mokhtar keeps the common threads from country to country. Any drummer interested in a fresh look at how to orchestrate a groove on the drumset would find these rhythms uplifting, and that's the idea, its all up!"

CHRIS PARKER, "Each groove is a dance and until you dance the patterns, they may seem daunting. Dance first and read the notes after then the grooves will explode. The first time you make that connection it will feel incredible."

BILLY MARTIN, "Finally, a book that includes North African rhythms. Thank you, Mokhtar. Respect!"

Bilingual English/Français
MIM002 $24.95

MOKHTAR SAMBA
AFRICAN RHYTHMS
AND INDEPENDENCE FOR DRUMSET
FROM THE EXPLOSIVE MOROCCAN-SENEGALESE DRUMMER OF YOUSSOU N'DOUR, SALIEF KEITA, CARLINHOS BROWN, RICHARD BONA, JEAN-LUC PONTY, ULTRAMARINE...
EDITED BY DAN THRESS
CD INCLUDED
BILINGUAL ENGLISH/FRANÇAIS

TONY MARTUCCI, "A welcome addition to the drumming lexicon. Ancient rhythms with endless modern day applications. Mokhtar's material not only opens doors of insights into his music, but that of jazz and Latin, as well as any form of creative popular music. Bravo!"

ROYAL HARTIGAN, "Mohktar has given us many creative and original adaptations of traditional African drumming styles. He presents the material in a logical order which allows us to develop each rhythmic element gradually, internalizing these difficult and multilayered patterns. His contribution highlights the sophistication, genius, and deep feeling in traditional African music."

DAVE STANOCH, "Roots rhythms made fresh, challenging and fun! Talk about coming full circle—by embracing the past— Mokhtar points us in the direction of the drumset's future!"

ALAIN RIEDER, "For a long time I had hoped an African drummer would write a book based on contemporary African drumset playing. Mokhtar did it, and what a drummer! His book is a gem."

ALBERTO SEMENZATO, "This man can really play! Many new books are just older books with an added CD. This book is a fresh, genuine project that will become a classic!"

MODERN DRUMMER, "As Mokhtar Samba explains in the introduction to this excellent book, there were no drumset players in African bands as recently as fifteen years ago. But by now an African kit tradition has been established, and Samba—who's played with, among others, Youssou N'Dour and Jean-Luc Ponty—takes the clearest, most direct route toward explaining it to a new audience."

THE ART OF PLAYING TIMBALES VOL 1
by VICTOR RENDON

A Complete Guide for Developing Rhythms, Solos and Traditional Timbale Techniques. Includes Drumset Adaptations, Conga and Bongo Transcriptions, Play-Along Charts, and Full Length CD.

VICTOR RENDÓN is a sought after New York City percussionist who is co-leader of The Latin Jazz Orchestra, and sideman with Mongo Santamaria, Chico O'Farrill, Carlos "Patato" Valdéz, Ray Santos, Grupo Caribe, The Latin Jazz Coalition, Los Más Valientes and many others. Rendón's work has appeared in Modern Drummer, DRUM!, Percussive Notes, and Warner Bros. Publications.

This excellent book and CD package is designed for the beginning timbalero, or drumset player, who wants to understand how to play Afro-Cuban music in a professional setting. If you have just purchased a pair of timbales, this book will teach you everything from proper setup, stick sizes, rhythms, independence, transitions, song forms, and SOLOING.

Each music example has a corresponding track number which can be found on the CD. Simply read the music exercises, and listen to the corresponding track number on your CD player. A complete Afro-Cuban percussion work-out. Each exercise on timbales is also arranged for drumset. Conga and bongo students will find their parts in each section of the book and CD. Please note: to take full advantage of this book, students are encouraged to learn each part for timbales, drumset, congas, and bongos.

Each section features play-along CHARTS and CD TRACKS with some of NY's top Latino musicians: Sergio Rivera (piano), Victor Venegas (bass), Heriberto Rivera (bongo), Aníbal "Tito" Rivera (congas), and Victor Rendón (timbales and drumset). By using these play-along charts you will gain valuable realistic playing experience that will directly translate to your school ensemble or professional group.

CHAPTERS: Introduction, Position of the Timbales, Different Sounds, Clave, Abanico, Cha Cha Chá, Son, Transitions, Bell Patterns, 6/8, Independence, Mozambique, Solo Phrases, References.

ALSO INCLUDED: INTERVIEWS with famous timbaleros: MIKE COLLAZO (Tito Rodriguez, Celia Cruz, Eddie Palmieri, Tito Puente), JOSE MADERA (Machito, Fania All-Stars, Pacheco, Tito Puente), and JOHNNY ALMENDRA (Jóvenes del Barrio, Willie Colón, Mongo Santamaria, John Scofield).

And SOLO TRANSCRIPTIONS from GUILLERMO BARRETO ("Descarga Cubana" from Cuban Jam Sessions in Miniature Descargas) and MANNY OQUENDO ("Llora Timbero" from Conjunto Libre Ritmo Sonido Estilo).

Bilingual: English/Español
MIM003 $24.95

MODERN DRUMMER, "Victor Rendon has done the improbable: He has made it possible for a wide range of drummer/percussionists to approach the art of timbales without fear of failure. Rendon breaks down the daunting clave structure so that we all can relate, and demonstrates how the instruments of the Afro-Cuban percussion section (timbales, congas, bongos, and sometimes drumset) function as a unit. Learning to play timbales (or to emulate their rhythms on drumset) makes any drummer more valuable on the bandstand, and Rendon's instructional method is as clear as it's going to get. The author's clarity in presentation is further enriched by his discussion of the evolution of Latin rhythms and instruments, and by his richly detailed interviews with master timbaleros. Victor Rendon has worked with giants like Mongo Santamaria and Patato Valdes, and has taught music for years within the New York community, and now he's authored the most authoritative book on the 'original' Latin drumkit. Viva timbales!"

VICTOR MENDOZA, "Victor has done a marvelous job laying it down at a basic level and within a very musical and realistic context. I particularly like the transition to the drumset. It's obvious that Victor is a great teacher as well as a great player. I will recommend it to the percussion faculty and students at the Berklee College of Music."

GORDON GOTTLIEB, "Victor Rendon's book is as close to having a virtual teacher by your side as one could get. Excellent photos of stick and hand positions, beautiful layout and clear instrument/sticking/hand notation key, independence exercises, transitions from paila to mambo bell, two solo transcriptions with recommended stickings and keys to phrasing it's *all* here. Percussionists and drummers are going to love this book. Destined to be a classic."

MIGUEL ANGÁ DIAZ: ANGÁ MANIA!
Percussion Video of the Year—DRUM! Magazine 2000

Miguel "Anga" Diaz (1961-2006) will be remembered as one of the greatest congueros of all time. Known for his remarkable soloing and multiple conga/percussion inventions, Cuban-born Diaz, represents the link between the past, present, and the future of conga playing. Now you can learn his techniques from this exclusive DVD masterclass.

Through a methodology based in tradition, Anga demonstrates many of his systems and forms he uses to develop dexterous patterns, riffs and solos. Each example is demonstrated in a solo context then in a duet performance. In the MARCHA, GUAGUANCO and SOLOING sections Anga reveals his incomparable patterns and variations on five congas. Duet performances with virtuoso Cuban pianist GABRIEL HERNANDEZ help illustrate Anga's ideas while he breaks-down his soloing phrases, playing each slowly and explaining the origin of each riff.

In the MIXING STLYLES section, Anga overdubs three layers of different drumming styles, mixing funk with the Cuban rhythms known as Pilon and Batumbata. He also shows how congas can bring an organic feel to the DJ-based styles such as jungle in duets with DJ GILB-R and an improvised trio segment featuring Anga playing his 'Set Cubano' mixing congas, bells, and drums (with both hands and feet) to create a phenomenal flow of rhythm.

MODERN DRUMMER, "Miguel "Angá" Diaz certainly knows conga traditions, but his flame burns brightest when breaking down barriers and mixing styles."

DRUM!, "In demonstrating solo and duet techniques in funk and jungle as well as traditional styles, Diaz comes out of the gate with five congas and never looks back."

LATIN PERCUSSIONIST, "Perhaps what makes this video different from others is that it deals with three, four, and five drum applications. Recommended."

CUSTOMER, "I knew it was only a matter of time until people found out about the best congero in the world!"

CUSTOMER, "The information is well explained and the camera angles allow you to see how the conga golpes (hits) are struck on each skin."

CUSTOMER, "This video is a great accomplishment especially the transcription booklet of Anga's playing. It helps all of out here who can follow it to improve our understanding of good latin conga playing."

Bilingual English/Español
MIM004 $29.95